THROUGH DEATH TO REBIRTH

TRUTH GLIMPSED ✦ FLAMES WITH *LIVING IDEAS* ✦
HONORED ONLY BY APPLYING THEM IN DAILY LIFE ✦
THIS IS THE PATH TO CONSCIOUS IMMORTALITY

Growth of the Soul

THROUGH DEATH

TO

REBIRTH

by

JAMES SCUDDAY PERKINS

Vice-President of The Theosophical Society

Adyar, Madras, India

THE THEOSOPHICAL PRESS

WHEATON, ILLINOIS

THROUGH DEATH TO REBIRTH

Copyright © 1961 by The Theosophical Press

First Edition.

LIBRARY OF CONGRESS CATALOG CARD NUMBER: 61—13301

Printed in the United States of America.

CONTENTS

THE ILLUSTRATIONS   ✌   ✌   *by the author*

9

The aeonian unfoldment of spirit through form, consciousness through matter, is symbolized in this drawing. The five-pointed star in the upper part of the design represents the Will of the manifested Creator. An individual Spark of His Divine Fire is indicated by the small star shown in the winged figure just beneath the star. This individualized Spark of Eternal Spirit is embodied in the form of the Immortal Soul — the winged figure. The Soul's immortal purpose is growth to godhood. There is an age-long preparation prior to the birth of the individualized soul. The Spirit has brooded over and nurtured a developing unit of consciousness that has evolved through the mineral, vegetable and animal kingdoms.

In the drawing these are symbolized by the crystal, the rose and the deer. At last a chalice of consciousness has been prepared for individualization by the Divine Spirit. It is at this stage that the human soul is born, as explained in the text, and then begins the long series of reincarnations of this Immortal Self in human bodies. Man is Spirit, Soul and Body, in that order of reality. The ages of struggle to evolve human bodies into sensitive harmonized vehicles for spiritual consciousness is the struggle of each individual soul to master in time every force and form with which he must cope in the lower worlds.

The drawing's elliptical character suggests the individual movement of consciousness from *centers above,* of Soul and Spirit, to *centers below,* of action, feeling and thought and vice versa: always from positive to positive pole across a negative field. Thus the spiritual will in man, represented by the tiny five-pointed star is the upper positive pole that together with the lower positive pole — the tiny star in the physical body — forms an ellipse across the negative field of the emotional world. Awareness of the movement of consciousness in elliptical rhythms between the Inner Self and the outer man engaged in daily activities is indicative of an awakening to what is immortal and what is not within one's self. Immortality is not a gift bestowed but an achievement won through individual effort. Always unlocked is the door through which man can walk forth by his own exertions into the freedoms of immortality.

6. THE SOUL RADIATES FROM THE CENTER..*page* 33

The illustration attempts to suggest a four dimensional reality — the within-withoutness of matter and consciousness — in a two dimensional drawing. One must grasp at once that the smallest area, the circle at the center, is identical with the infinite beyond shown outside all of the circles. The figure at the center is the same figure as the largest one drawn with dotted line in the *spiritual beyond*. As shown, the mental plane envelops and permeates the emotional world, or astral plane; similarly both enfold and penetrate the physical plane. Hence the physical plane is seen here as the shut-in world of utmost limitation. The soul center is beyond the lower and *in* the higher, mental world. The pen line drawing conveys the idea of a reincarnating soul radiating energies from the center to create mental, astral and physical bodies. These bodies are outer encasements of a soul, or more precisely understood, they are vehicles for a soul's action in the three lower worlds. The complete physical incarnation is represented by the four small figures of the child, youth, adult and aged man. The integrated performance of soul and bodies during an incarnation develops an entity, a living personality, of character, appearance and general conduct, by which we recognize the person. After death the Soul withdraws step by step to its center as it dissociates its higher life from the denser forms.

This arrangement is a reminder that the currently recognized historical records of man and his evolution from theorized origins do not provide sufficient time for a reasonable hypothesis of the evolution of individual consciousness by means of reincarnation. The adoption of the theory of reincarnation requires the positing of vaster epochs of civilized human life on earth.

Shown here is a natural posture for meditation through the practice of which consciousness can be focused for inward exploration as described beginning on page 41.

Exploring the atom with the human microscope focused through the lens of knowledge and imagination. The procedure is elaborated on pages 45 and 46.

The man who has even a general theosophical

knowledge of the realms he will dwell in after death possesses a very valuable map. It will enable him to recognize where he is and in what direction he is going. Such knowledge also will help him to render understanding help to others. The illustration charts the normal course taken after death through the shadowy etheric portion of the physical plane, and on through the astral and heaven worlds, reaching those regions of universality at the height of the inward cycle wherein dwells the Soul in his causal body.

The little sketch tells the story: suddenly one steps outside the physical body aware that there is nothing to fear about departure from the physical world. Familiar surroundings may be perfectly visible but it is usually futile to try to communicate with friends present there, as is explained in the text.

The whole experience is that of looking up, stepping up, moving onward, out of the earth life now ended. As illustrated, the old man, long a cripple, dies clutching his worn crutch. He is aided by an invisible helper to release the physical body and walk into the Light as the vigorous young person he knows himself to be within, casting aside the unnecessary astral crutch.

Wrapped in the fiery cocoon of his own desires

even after dying from his physical body, the person who is trying to cling to material forms as pictured will be earthbound for as long as his passionate desires are stronger than the tidal forces that draw him into the normal stream of the after death cycle. The large hand shown at the top of the drawing is representative of the reality of the Soul's power to break through the illusory cocoon and beckon the returning individual to resume progress inward to the Soul's deep center.

Depicted is the bewildering and unhappy situation of the person who has fled physical entanglement via the suicide route. He is in the gray etheric world where temporarily there is no surcease from the repetitive emotions, fiery thoughts and phantom forms that compelled his act. Once more the Soul's beneficent power with its light shining from within is suggested by the hand in a gesture of blessing. In due time this inner Light will break through and release the Soul from imprisonment.

This drawing was conceived as illustrative of the experiencing of sudden death by one who is absorbed at the time in nobler contemplations and reverence for life, and who is instantly transported into a universe of Light where death is not known. The individual who suddenly encounters death through some violent accident will discover that he is immediately conscious in realms where he already abides in his inner life. As a man lives within himself so does he die. Those whose earth lives have been orderly, dutiful and kindly have no affinity for gruesome atmospheres and are oblivious of the surroundings of the fatal accident in which their physical bodies are destroyed.

16. HEAVEN IS INEVITABLE ....*page* 101

The Soul is projected into incarnation in the form of his alter ego, the human personality. Death of the latter in stages marks the Soul's return to his realm; thus his "going to heaven" is inevitable. The drawing is symbolic of the harmonized union of the eternal masculine-feminine polarities, the soul and personality, in heaven. The episodes between incarnations of this divine love affair in heaven are a refreshing preparation for rebirth. Human consciousness becomes focused for another incarnation in earthly existence where the masculine and feminine elements are polarities that ever hunger for union in their polar opposites. The five-pointed star symbolizes the Divine Spirit enfolding and blessing the heavenly reunion of Self.

17. VISION OF THE IMMORTAL TASK ....*page* 107

The painting represents man's recapture of soul-vision amidst his earthly experiences — awakening to his immortal task. In the sublime regions where between incarnations the Soul dwells in a vision of the Eternal Plan, he is renewed with divine purpose that will be tried in the fires below. As shown in the illustration, man strives forward and upward through the ordeals of life resisting the drag downward by the elemental forces innate in lower forms of matter, and assisted by the radiant subtle forces of nature surrounding him. Behind and within him (depicted as the shining triangle) are the powers of the Immortal Self raying forth his Will, Love and Creative Intelligence.

At the appointed hour — for this is a universe of law — the Soul's descent into incarnation begins. The illustration symbolizes this intent with the pointing hand through which is shown the flowing force activating the permanent atoms retained in lower worlds, around which are built mental, astral and physical bodies for reincarnation. The action is described on page 109.

Pictured is the operation of the universal law of action and reaction. Every thought, emotion and desire, as well as every act, is a force: a cause set in motion, whose effect returns upon its creator bringing in just measure the good or ill that was meted out originally. As suggested in the illustration, each of us stands in the hand of the Divine Creator, each strewing his path of daily life with seeds and stones of good and evil. The Eternal Law acts to accumulate these causes — the stones into great boulders of limitation along the Soul's path into the future, and the seeds of good acts that grow as blossoms of Beauty and nourishing Truth along the way. Every soul is involved in the harvests of the past while sowing the seeds of future harvests.

The Soul is illustrated here as a blindfolded infant

because he returns to earth through the waters of forgetfulness and arrives with little power to control the three new bodies, mental, astral and physical, represented as the elephant, tiger and horse respectively. He is handed the reins of control by an angelic figure that represents the workers in invisible kingdoms who were active in the building of the Soul's new vehicles.

Through repeated plunges into the abyss of matter, each individual in his own world of the real and unreal seeks the inner Light. As he discovers and evokes the Light amidst his experiences, he develops spiritual skills by means of which he progresses toward liberation from the cycle of necessity — freedom from the need to reincarnate.

As shown, the position of the seated human figure has a spatial configuration suggestive of two interlaced equilateral triangles. In such form the triangles symbolize the union of the mortal and divine natures of man. In the design the lines radiating outward from the head suggest the creative forces that are awakened through self-illumination. The worlds of form that have been harmonized and mastered are represented by the triple lotus bed upon which the perfected man is seated in repose enjoying the bliss of "Bright-Day" forever as he takes up the greater tasks of superhuman creation.

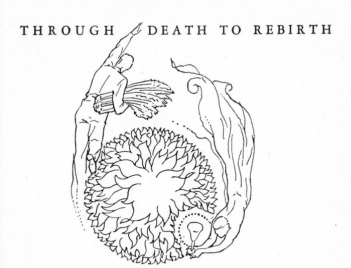

INTRODUCTORY

There are a number of excellent volumes on Theosophy containing information about the subjects of life after death and reincarnation. For the reader's convenience some of these books are indicated and recommended for further investigation. The present writing is offered in the hope of encouraging wider interest in this field of knowledge so charged with vital ideas and fresh direction for the modern mind. The direction is toward an awakened awareness of *living immortally now*, a creative and joyous outlook that may be denoted as "conscious immortality."

In a number of ways, what is called objective reality gives rise to crystallized ideas that are deadening, rather than life-giving, because they bind man's consciousness to that which perishes. Various expressions such as the famous words of Shakespeare in *Hamlet*, wherein reference is made to the grave as "that bourne from which no traveler returns," have had undue influence perhaps, in shaping people's day-to-day attitudes toward death. A distinction is made here between what are referred to as *living* ideas — ideas that release the powers of the Immortal Self — and those ideas that confine consciousness in material form, completely identifying it with matter and thereby pointing to its extinction with the disintegration of the form. From this standpoint modern scientific knowledge may be said to support philosophies of death rather than of life, because it is a knowledge that emphasizes mortal values; the prevailing view being that man's consciousness arises from his physical body and vanishes with its dissolution, as some collective coinage, so to speak, of the realm of brain, nerves and glands. Concepts of man's nature that are derived from sensate knowledge are oriented to perishability, pointing to the survival and welfare of the earthly self as the overruling objectives in life. With that outlook, any ideas about what happens to the individual when his body dies will, by their very nature, tend to draw consciousness toward a vortex of isolation and aloneness which in fact characterizes death.

Living ideas, on the other hand, move the individual consciousness toward participation in life's united *Wholeness* — toward imperishability and inexhaustible creativity. A person's freedom or imprisonment in matter, therefore, is dependent upon his motivating ideas. Freed through living ideas, his consciousness dissolves iron chains and soars beyond the mightiest bastions of stone and earth. He can wing his way in ever widening spheres of liberated being that will merge at last in universality and ultimate union with the Supreme. Living ideas lead the individual into realms that are native to the Immortal Self or Soul in man.

A recognition of these realities has provided the background for the following glimpses of the journey through death to rebirth.

DEATH A FAMILIAR EXPERIENCE

It requires but a moment's reflection to perceive that death is a constant companion, a familiar experience to all of us, living as we do amidst death within ourselves all the time. The very tissues of our bodies are in a continual state of renewal, their basic units, the cells, dying and being rebuilt every hour of the day and night. The physical body itself remains alive and efficiently functioning, because this process of rebirth amidst death is ceaselessly restoring it and adjusting it to changing demands.

Similarly our emotional bodies are undergoing continuous changes that are of the nature of death and rebirth. The emotional body is a structure of feelings generated by relationships and circumstances that are at all times in a state of flux. However firmly the emotional body may be poised upon deeply felt personal convictions of truth and right, of loving hopes so poignantly inspired, of sympathies and attachments affectionately held, inevitable readjustments must occur. Stresses bend feelings into new shapes; time encrusts them in unanticipated moulds, while fresh experiences may entirely replace wide areas of feeling. Sometimes, as we know, shock can bring the whole emotional structure crashing about our ears to our despair. In such light then, the emotional body can be viewed in perspective as continually experiencing rebirth amidst death.

Cannot the same be said of the mental body —

that is to say, of one's structure of thought, ideas and knowledge? This structure does not remain the same. Old ideas are dying, new ones coming to birth every day; and over a period of years our mental vehicles are changed enormously in response to the evolving world environment. The rapid advances in modern communications systems alone are making evident the swift altering of our mental bodies. One has only to recollect the world as it was before television and radio broadcasting to realize the extent of changes in outlook that these developments have brought about. We know that we have but to press a button to participate in various experiences of communication, entertainment and instruction that were never before available in such wealth. Even the singing commercials in American broadcasts urging in lyrical tunes the purchase of various objects and nostrums are changing mass patterns of thought and ideas. When we remember that before 1945 only technically minded people with specialized interests sought knowledge about the atomic structure of physical matter, while the rest of us could safely ignore the subject, we see one of the most startling changes in world-wide thought. For no one can have an informed opinion upon matters that spell the difference between life and death for all of us without having at least some basic knowledge of such an abstruse subject as the composition of the atom's nucleus. So it is readily discernible that our mental bodies are subject to constant change by cultural impacts, and that mental adjustments are continually demanded of everyone if he is to preserve a healthy state of equilibrium. Just as in the physical and emotional bodies, the mental form, too, survives all vicissitudes and remains vital and vigorously growing, only because of the transformations that are indicated here as rebirth amidst death.

BODIES CONTINUOUSLY DYING

The cycle of death and rebirth, therefore, is common to all three bodies, mental, emotional and physical. Death and rebirth are two phases of a single cycle, rebirth being the other half of death. A person dies to be reborn. He dies from childhood to become the youth, and from youth to become the mature adult, and finally he dies from maturity into old age. Yet throughout all the cyclic changes there is an unbroken continuity of consciousness. Everyone is clear that he is the same person whose life so many years ago was that of the child, and is now a new edition of himself. Self-identity is preserved despite all modifications that occur. In a similar way self-identity continues through the changes beyond the body's death. What is more important to know is that an extension of self-identity, to include the element in our nature that is immortal, can result in experiences of *conscious immortality* now. This state of self-enlightenment is approached through projecting one's thought repeatedly toward that region of one's inner being, the imperishable or Higher Self, as one does in meditation; and with sustained practice, rendering the excursion into subtler worlds a familiar experience. Required is certain basic knowledge of man's invisible nature and latent powers.

BASIS FOR IMMORTALITY

The more comprehensive view of man's nature afforded by Theosophy begins with the concept that all life emerges from *within*, that is to say, from the higher region termed *spiritual*. This reverses the scientific speculation that life

has some physical origin. From a theosophical position, an individual's higher principles that compose his spiritual being are the greater reality
when compared with his transitory physical body.
This idea of emergence from within that is derived from theosophical studies of the origin of
the universe as well as of humanity, is the key to
an understanding of man's nature, as well as the
meaning and purpose of life's creation. The central theme of Theosophy's framework of synthesis is the seven-fold nature of the universe and
of man.* It will be helpful to the following dis-
cussion if this central conception be kept in mind.
The physical world is but the outermost envelope
of matter, or spirit-matter, in seven stages of
densification. Matter is permeated with universal
energy, or Spirit, the two being not only united
but interchangeable when stepped down from
higher to lower levels, or vice versa. The seven
vast energy levels that include all of life and its
forms are the seven planes of nature that extend
from the sublest regions of Divine Consciousness
to the densest physical matter.

In man's cycle of death and rebirth we are
concerned principally with the three lower of
these planes: the *physical plane* which is fully per-

The Ancient Wisdom, by Annie Besant

ceived; the invisible emotional world usually referred to as the *astral plane,* because its matter is luminous when compared to physical matter; and the *mental plane* where thoughts take shape. In every level or plane of manifestation, the inner Self of man expresses life through the outermost encasement. When the outer body is physical, the invisible thoughts and feelings are given expression through physical activities. But if the consciousness is removed from the physical world, and the astral body becomes the outer vehicle, the thoughts and feelings are expressed through that body in the astral world which is as substantial to a person there as the physical world is to him here. In a similar manner, when the outer vehicle is mental, the consciousness is experiencing life through that medium.

Theosophy postulates that the deep center in every man is a Fragment of Divine Consciousness, his imperishable Spirit or Monad, as it is termed, because that word signifies unity, or a unit. Innate with purpose, this inmost Self radiates his life outward into the denser planes of matter in order to awaken his latent divine nature. This unfoldment requires experience in the physical, astral and mental worlds, enduring their conditions and responding to them in ways that call into manifestation the hidden realities of his nature.

A rapid glance at the mighty pilgrimage of evolution begins with the first objective, which is to establish in the lower kingdoms of nature a firm center of consciousness that will survive all vicissitudes and become in time an enduring link between highest spirit and the densest forms of matter. Progress in the direction of this achievement moves in stages or cycles of development, first in lower kingdoms of nature, and at length in the higher animal kingdom, when the evolving unit of consciousness reaches a stage of preparation for advancement into the human kingdom, becoming thereby "individualized."* This gigantic leap forward in evolution takes place when, at the lawful and appropriate time, an animal consciousness that in some hour of need is aspiring upward with transcendent effort, experiences an overshadowing of the Monad who flashes forth his life in fiery radiance to unite the animal's consciousness with Divine Spirit, an act that thereby creates an *immortal soul.*

Knowledge of the sublime purpose underlying aeonian evolution sheds a great light of understanding upon the birth and nature of the human Soul. Above all, it reveals that the Soul is not

*First Principles of Theosophy, Chapter VII, by C. Jinarajadasa

BASIS FOR IMMORTALITY

some misty, shadowy appurtenance of man's physical reality, but a radiant center of Power, Love and Intelligence established in its own locale in a specific body of subtlest mental matter. Herein the Soul resides in its vehicle which is given the name *causal body.** Its destiny is to unfold its latent divinity through experiencing incarnations in human stages of evolution. Born in time, then, the Soul is beyond death, being of the nature of the Eternal. Growth is made possible by the rhythmic cycles of reincarnation in which the Soul, as a peerless chalice of virtue, extracts the good and the true from every experience encountered in its journey toward perfection. Life after life it moves from one race to another, incarnating in the various nations and civilizations of mankind, and the joys and trials, the battles fought and victories won, all take place in the arena of the Soul. The end result of all this effort is that the Divine Spirit incarnate in the Soul, unfolds His triune being of omnipresence, omniscience and omnipotence, and another Son of God enters his Divine Heritage.

This brief explanation, amplified by deeper study of the processes mentioned here, furnishes the substantial basis for realizing that an aware-

*The Causal Body, by A. E. Powell

ness of *conscious immortality* is not only possible but will certainly arrive in due season with the growth of the Soul. Further, it renders realistic St. Paul's listing of the elements of man's whole being as spirit, soul and body, in that order if first things are placed first.

THE SOUL RADIATES FROM THE CENTER

With even a glimpse of this sweeping panorama of the purpose and meaning of man's life on earth, we are able to observe that each cycle does not begin with the birth of the baby's body; it begins before birth in the realms of the Soul, when that Central Intelligence determines upon a new incarnation. Then at the appointed hour the Soul's energies radiate outward through the three lower spheres of matter, the mental, astral and physical, putting on three "coats of skin," or bodies of the matter of each of those planes, the densest physical vehicle being the outer, visible body, permeated and enveloped by the subtler matter of the invisible astral and mental bodies. It may be found helpful to visualize this situation of the whole self as a series of concentric spheres with the Source of life radiating consciousness from the center through the mental and astral spheres to the physical ring where it is focused for the lifetime on earth. This is expressed in graphic form by the illustration on the opposite page, which should be given careful scrutiny. It is intended to convey the fourth dimensional effect of a higher, *spiritual beyond* that is simultaneously at the center of one's being and at large in the universe, thus being both within and without the confining lower bodies. The mental and astral worlds surround and permeate the physical world shown here as the densest and darkest region. In the physical world the four figures representing childhood, youth, adulthood and old age are shown as illustrating the span of a single reincarnation on earth. When life terminates, and the physical body dies, consciousness recedes in stages toward its Source center. It has of necessity to become dissociated from its recent involvement in physical matter. This purgation process takes place in the astral world where the nature of desiring and feeling that developed during the past earth life undergoes reconditioning and refining that permit, at length, the further withdrawal of consciousness into the mental or "heaven world." The discarnate Soul now becomes completely freed of investiture in lower matter. The harvest of his life's experience is translated into spiritual

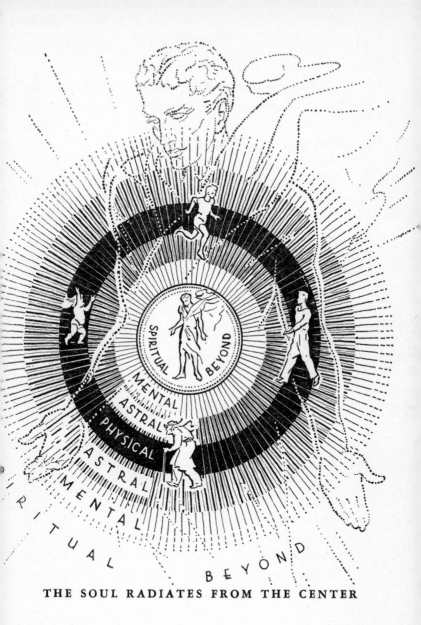

THE SOUL RADIATES FROM THE CENTER

capacity, into added faculties and growth of the Soul, as preparation for a return to earth centuries hence in a future reincarnation. A person does not, therefore, die from the physical world to "go to heaven." Rather the Immortal Soul which has come forth from the highest heaven into incarnation in the three lower worlds of matter — three states of consciousness — to labor and create in matter, to experience its impacts, to endure and to struggle for mastery of force and form, retires homeward for refreshment. The focal center of the Self is there, not here. *The earth is the "bourne" from which every traveler returns* to his native land, the realm of the Soul.

WE LIVE IN THREE WORLDS SIMULTANEOUSLY

Self-awareness implies full alertness of the inner Self to the three worlds of form that are being experienced simultaneously in the co-existence of the three bodies, physical, emotional and mental, as a single selfhood. Everyone is aware of the physical vestment, how to use it and move about in it. At the same time that we are acting, we feel and desire in the emotional, or astral, body. If we're also thinking objectively, the mental body, likewise, is brought into action.

All of us are normally functioning in this manner — acting in three different worlds even though the impacts and responses at all three levels reach final acknowledgement and expression through the physical body and brain. An important point to note is that the three bodies are being individually evolved in time through adaptation to environment, under the law of cause and effect, the harvests of one cycle of incarnation being inherited as seeds of potentiality in the next cycle. Thus an expanded theory of evolution can account for certain voids in modern man's knowledge about himself.

No one doubts the theory of physical evolution; collected evidence overwhelmingly supports it. But there is no recognition given, nor can there be any scientific support, as yet, for the theory that each man inherits from himself his individually evolved emotional and mental capacities; that he is the recipient of acquired characteristics developed in previous lifetimes on earth. Certain evidence does suggest such a theory. Obviously there are higher and lower strata of emotional and mental responses to life. There are, for example, primitive tribes on earth where a top cultural event will be a barbaric tribal dance around some jungle fire; while, that same evening, in some modern city, other groups of people are gathered to enjoy a symphony, or a metaphysical discourse. As offered here, these dissimilarities of interest and response are illustrative of differing stages of evolution in individual emotional and mental bodies, and not simply due to chance differences of environment. In general, people are located where they are because they are compelled to be there by forces arising out of their past evolutional history. Dissimilar faculties are not accounted for, reasonably, by difference of environment, opportunity, and physical heredity alone.

This field of investigation calls for another Charles Darwin whose attention will be given to the subtler realms of nature, collecting and classifying data obtained in emotional and mental worlds as evidence supporting such an extension of the theory of evolution. In a significant measure, theosophical investigators have approached such research and have collected evidence of other existing streams of evolution in invisible worlds that parallel physical evolution. A serious consideration of what has been found with respect to man and his subtler vehicles urges recognition of reincarnation and laws that govern its operation.

The concept of reincarnation meets its greatest stumbling block in the present-day acceptance of recorded history as final and authoritative with respect to the dating of earliest human cultural developments. But recorded histories fail to provide sufficient time to entertain sensibly the idea of *reincarnational heredity,* or the individual inheritance of characteristics acquired as a result of past action in other lives. A good example of the problem presented in this respect is revealed by investigations of the time elapsing between incarnations on earth. It has been found through clairvoyant research that normally a cultivated person of today has not been in incarnation on earth for approximately a thousand or twelve hundred years; and that in all likelihood he will not be reborn for about a thousand years in the future. Therefore, he is at the midpoint of a cycle that has a span of about two thousand years. He is directly linked to all three of these lifetimes, in that he is working out situations and coping with forces that were created, or given momentum, in his last life; while in his present life, he is releasing new forces, that will affect the character and conditions of his next life. All this is happening through his activities now. This wider frame of outlook extends his immediate existence across many centuries of time. It appears at once that only a few of those two-thousand-year spans would account for all of historical time, beginning with the early records of about twelve or fifteen thousand years ago. From a reincarnational point of view, the whole of the period of recorded history is only a fragment of the time that is required to evolve a highly intellectual, cultivated man of today. Anthropologists, at present, trace the origins of a creature recognizable as man as far back as five hundred thousand years. If this is factual, is it not unreasonable to suppose that for approximately four hundred and ninety thousand years mankind existed in the most primitive condition and then suddenly, in relatively recent times, leaped forward in evolution and began creating, in a number of scattered places on earth, advanced stages of civilization? This illogical picture of man's past could be clarified if the more reasonable theory of evolution through reincarnation were adopted. Then it would be perceived that all of the four hundred and ninety thousand years, and millions* more besides, are needed to account for the evolution of modern man's individual consciousness; it would make sense that ages of time, and unnumbered civilizations and cultures must have arisen and fallen, through which individuals have had to pass, to unfold the faculties and capacities of a William Shakespeare, a Leonardo da Vinci, an Albert Einstein!

Modern sciences are based on the data of sensate knowledge, that is, the recording, classifying and analyzing of observations registered upon one or another of the five senses of a human being. However delicate and refined the physical tools and instruments may become for observing, weighing and measuring, all these have finally to be recorded with the sensory faculties of some investigator. The fixed assumption that cements all perception is that the facts and laws of nature are discerned and can be recorded by man's brain and sensory equipment alone. When the human

---

*See *The Secret Doctrine* (Adyar Edition 1938) by H. P. Blavatsky, Vol. 3, Chapter on "The History of The Fourth Race," particularly pp. 252, 253, 263. Esoteric philosophy states that physical man has been in evolution on this planet for approximately 18,000,000 years.

WITH KNOWLEDGE ... *explore inwardly*

physical apparatus perishes, nothing remains —
consciousness itself being but a stream of effluent
phenomena arising from or accompanying physical functions. Death of the physical form is the
end of all. Since there have been no machines
invented that record, predictably and efficiently,
creature activity and phenomena occurring in the
astral and mental worlds, there can be no ac-
credited sciences that explore beyond the regions
of sensate responses. And yet, even the materialist
who may ponder the subject of death strictly from
the standpoint of scientific experimental knowledge, has of necessity, it would seem, to posit the
survival and continuance of consciousness beyond
the dissolution of the physical body. Such cogi-
tation might be dramatized and made visual in
the following way.

PERCEPTIVE USE OF IMAGINATION

A perceptive exercise using imaginatively whatever knowledge you have of physiology, biology, chemistry, psychology and physics may
be arranged as a form of meditation. You may
begin by visualizing the whole physical body,
passing in thought swiftly over its exterior, and
then direct consciousness to sink through the sur-

face of the skin, through the dermis and epi-
dermis, and on inward, past the tiny nerve endings
and blood vessels, into the world of muscles,
bones and organs. There, you may center attention
upon the marvellous organization of the physical
body, using your knowledge of physiology to
examine the blood stream with its many vital
functions, and the nervous system and glandular
apparatus. Journeying onward, with the aid of
biology, you may explore the vast commonwealth
of cells that are active throughout the body. These
billions of tiny builders are gathered in special
communities of brain cells, muscle cells, bone
cells, and so on — all of them constituting a particular stream of evolution of their own. Now,
with a further demand upon knowledge and
imagination, focus awareness within the walls of
a single cell, observing its jelly-like mass of proto-
plasm throbbing with a mysterious rhythm that
suggests attunement with the ebb and flow of
universal forces. Enthralling vistas open in this
direction, but without being deflected from the
course of this exercise, proceed to the next stage
by resolving your viewpoint microscopically to
look into the very substance of the cell itself,
watching it become ever more tenuous as you
diminish the range, until the substance resembles

clusters of stars in the Milky Way. Here, all resemblance to physical matter as recognized by the five senses disappears. The whirling points of light now in view are the fireworks display of the molecules composing the chemical elements of the cell.

Steadily sharpening the focus by thinking of the known composition of molecules, you may select a particular one and enter its strange, geometrically arranged world, with its dancing light-points surrounding you. Hurrying onward, now converging in a single light-point, aided by a knowledge of physics, you enter — the atom! Access to its world does not necessarily require force and explosive violence. We are seeing here the possibility of the atom's exploration silently and serenely by the focused will. Great occultists have testified to this possibility. The ultimate physical atom apparently is a sphere of forces holding back, or pushing outward against *primal substance* as might some empty bubble floating in the "waters of space."*

Venturing to continue this imaginative journey into the atom and its nucleus, you may visualize the relative proportions of space and nuclear par-

*See *Occult Chemistry*, Chapter I: *The Nature of Matter*, by Annie Besant and C. W. Leadbeater.

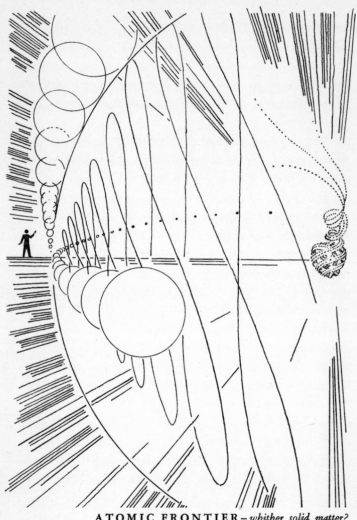

ATOMIC FRONTIER – *whither solid matter?*

ticles, in terms of present day scientific conceptions of the orbiting electrons and central nucleus. The picture-story has been graphically described as follows, with measurements based upon experimental knowledge: Supposing the Planetarium in Chicago to represent the nucleus of a hydrogen atom, you would have to imagine its one electron as being the size of a grapefruit orbiting the nucleus — the building in Chicago — in a path that curved across the center of Hudson Bay and down toward Newfoundland, to Key West, Florida, around via San Antonio, Texas, through Billings, Montana, and return. The area is colossal compared to the size of the particles. One's first impression of the inner spaces of the atom is that of awesome emptiness. Yet this first impression is illusory as we shall see. In the exploratory journey, you have arrived at the perimeter of the atom. From this point, gazing in wonderment toward the atom's far-off center, you behold a stupendous display of forces in motion, with no hint of spacious solitudes. The "bubble," is not empty! Indeed infinite spheres, each one a force field, seem to be active within the atom's circumference. Series of spheres, each composed of waves of force that spring from center and circumference simultaneously, are hurtling toward you at a tremendous velocity. They are dissolving one globe into another, instantaneously collapsing into ever smaller spheres as their centers approach the atom's perimeter in a beautiful path, curving from the atom's center to its circumference. The coalescing globes of force become points of energy and light as they merge with the spherical surface of the atom in fiery sparks that flash around the atomic perimeter at enormous speed and return to the point of "surfacing." Then they explode inward, the points of light again becoming globular, ever larger spheres whose surfaces are widening waves of force, and whose centers are tracing again the perfect arc from the atom's circumference to its center.

You are now located at the very heart of physical matter, observing the wave-point phenomena of the atomic particles — the atom's out-breathing of forces of radiation, and its in-breathing forces of gravitation. The wave centers appear from and disappear into the central nucleus, materializing and vanishing intermittently as though having no substantial existence in physical matter. If the observer moves into the nucleus itself, he is in a flaming vortex, a boiling mass, of electrical forces that are classified according to behaviour as the nuclear particles: protons, neutrons, mesons, etc.

Some of these materialize at highest velocity, release bundles of energy, and disappear through "reversed vortices," or holes in matter, into the zero region or zone of neutrality from whence they came.

This is the edge of the physical world.* Nuclear physicists assert that attempts to picture events in the atom's nucleus are useless, not to say impossible, and that all data can be recorded only in mathematical equations. If this is true, the material scientist is confronted with the necessity of conceiving that out of the sheer abstractions of mathematical points in space and force fields that shift and disappear, is derived your own solid appearance and that of the physical universe, your house and its walls, the continents and oceans, the planet and all the galaxies of stars.

WHERE IS SOLID REALITY?

Having arrived at this frontier of physical matter, surveying its illusory nature from an atomic viewpoint, one is compelled to ask: Where, now, is solid reality for the person who must see

*The picture is visualized with present day atomic data in mind, as well as the theosophical concepts of primordial substance and the vortical motion set up therein by the One Life that permeates the seven planes of the universe with neutral zones or "laya centers" between them.

and touch, weigh and measure everything, in order to accept it as real? In the realm of atoms there are no ultimate building blocks from which the world as we know it is constructed. Even the apparently firm perimeter of the physical body is continually fluctuating with changing situations and conditions. Atoms and their particles are flashing into, and out of, its arena. The physical body is an assemblage of force fields, its many energies affecting, and being affected by, the surrounding physical world. The bewildered observer must ask what magic, then, holds together the body's collective order, its myriads of atoms, each one a vast system; its countless billions of molecules, each a galaxy of atoms; its teeming hordes of cells that compose the tissues, organs, nerves, bones and skin of an athlete's — or dancer's — smoothly functioning body? What can that agency be but the evolving unit of human self-consciousness with its central primary triad of Power, Love and Intelligence — the Divine Fragment that was in existence before anything was created in this physical universe, and will be here imperishably when all else has disappeared?

With a deepened grasp upon the illusory character of the physical form, we are now in a position to address ourselves to the question:

WHAT IS DEATH?

The simplest answer, deriving from what has already been said, is that death is the final withdrawal of consciousness from its outermost form, the physical body. Tissues continue, as usual, to decompose, but they are no longer being repaired and replaced; organic material begins to disintegrate into chemical elements; molecules set off upon individual courses; atoms fly apart. And there, in one direction go the multitudes of particles and miscellaneous items that compose the body; while in another direction has disappeared the mysterious integrative power that united the whole, and governed the body's empire — the unit of consciousness, that, together with its higher principles, constitute the Immortal Soul. Does it too dissolve into nothingness as some cloud of vapor into thin air? With the death of the body, does consciousness lose its focus as an individual identity? Have the abilities and capacities that were developed out of a lifetime of effort disappeared forever, the whole of it but a tracing of vain, illusory hopes? What can we really know of an individual's situation after the physical body dies? More important, *can we follow the path of this unit of consciousness in its course beyond the grave?*

KNOWLEDGE ABOUT LIFE AFTER DEATH

It is a modern superstition that nothing can be known about our after-death states of being. There has always existed a definite body of knowledge about the superphysical regions that are entered at the time of death. Such information has been accumulating for ages from many sources. Studies of comparative ancient and modern sciences and religions have yielded rich stores of knowledge that have been further confirmed by direct observation through the use of powers that are latent in all men, and are awakened in some — powers such as extra-sensory perception, and even subtler kinds of direct knowing. This accumulated knowledge, together with its philosophical implications, constitutes what is termed the Ancient Wisdom of mankind. Taught in the Mystery Schools of Greece, Egypt and India, and through many other avenues, an elaborated synthesis of this knowledge is available today as Theosophy.* From this source may be derived a kind of mapping of the route which we follow upon leaving the physical world at death. A quick glance at the course ahead will assist us in examining in greater detail the passage through death and into the inner realms.

*The Ancient Wisdom by Annie Besant.

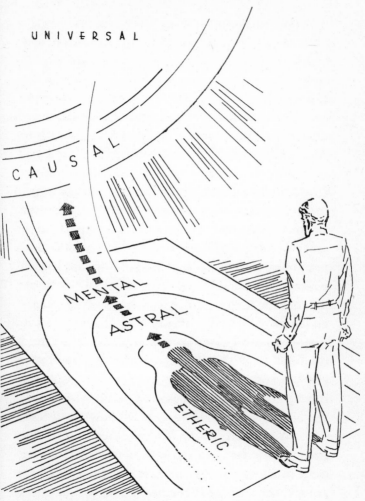

MAP OF THE AFTER-DEATH ROUTE

Scanning the map, as it were, our attention is first drawn to the fact that the transition after death, into the next world of consciousness, the Astral Plane, is accomplished by passage through the sheath of finest physical matter that has acted as a vital link between physical and higher levels of matter. This vehicle is known specifically as the *etheric double*,* because it duplicates the physical form in subtler physical matter. It has important functions of its own. There are, according to theosophical researches, seven grades of physical matter, viz: atomic, subatomic, super-etheric, etheric, gaseous, liquid, solid. The physical body is composed of all seven grades. However, there is a distinct division between the denser solid, liquid, gaseous portions of the vehicle and its subtler envelope consisting of the four finer levels of matter, that together are designated as the etheric double. This sheath surrounds and permeates every tissue and cell of the denser body. Coursing through it are the streams of vitality that keep the body alive and healthy. It is known by occultists that emanating from the sun there is a distinct force which has been recognized in India from ancient times as *prana*, a Sanskrit word derived from *pra* (forth), and *an* (Breathe), hence *pra-an* means

*The Etheric Double, by A. E. Powell

to breathe forth. This prana, or vitality is absorbed by the etheric double through its specialized equipment, and dispatched to every region of the body, energizing and vitalizing it through the centers that absorb and distribute it.* This is a phase of knowledge that can be helpful to those who are interested in subjects concerning the attainment of balanced health and harmony of life.

Upon death of the physical body, the normal passage of the individual's consciousness through after-death stages ignores the etheric double, relinquishing at once this sheath. (The passage will be given further attention later.) Following this, the period of life in the astral world commences. For some individuals the time spent there is brief, for others it is more extended. This is so because disentanglement from all desires and feelings that were identified with physical matter is undertaken in the astral world. Naturally the person, given to coarser sensual cravings and their gratifications, will require a longer time for disenthrallment. Eventually this is accomplished, and the astral period terminates. Following it, is passage into the mental, or heaven world, where the major period of time is spent by all people whose aspi-

*The Chakras, by C. W. Leadbeater

rations and pursuits have been less material. Educated, intelligent people of today are said to dwell in this region for a thousand years or more. During this longest after-death period, which is the closing phase of the total cycle of an incarnation, the soul of man reaps the full benefit of his recent lifetime on earth, preparing in due season, for the return known as reincarnation. Having glanced in this way at the chart of the after-death course, we are ready now for a more detailed description of the various stages that will be experienced.

THE EXPERIENCING OF DEATH

The first observation to be made about dying is that a person does not thereby simply cease to exist as the individual he has known himself to be; he does not enter an utterly strange and entirely unfamiliar condition. Rather his situation is a continuation of his present life in extended phases. Dying is very much the same experience as going to sleep, which everyone does during some portion of the twenty-four hour daily cycle. No healthy person is rendered uneasy or fearful by this routine demand. If our attitude toward going to sleep were analagous to the common superstitions about dying, there would be endless added fears and occasions for grief. Happily everyone is quite certain that he will wake up tomorrow morning. Is it not significant that one of the joys of life is that of becoming physically unconscious at regular intervals? We greet sleep amiably because of the anticipated renewal of strength and vitality. Sleep refreshes us, returning us to a state of well-being and eager interest in what is happening in the world about us and to us. It would be only reasonable to view death and rebirth as a larger cycle of refreshment and renewal. This would be the normal outlook if man's instinctive "soul-knowledge" about this matter were permitted to govern his attitudes, rather than the fears and beliefs that are instilled in him as a result of life's circumstances.

More people give the subject of death deeper consideration than is commonly believed. An interesting survey was conducted in nine scattered countries of the world in 1958, on the question of belief in life after death. It revealed that in six of the countries more than half of the population was convinced of the continuation of life beyond the grave. The proportion ranged from the high of 79% in one country to the low of 30% in another. In the latter country 46% were sure that there was no life after death, or not likely to be.* In all places the percentage of those with definite opinions one way or the other, indicates that much serious thought is being devoted to the subject. Not only thought, but intuition might be given more weight by all of us in arriving at convictions regarding this inevitable experience that everyone meets. A good example of the conflict between common thought and deeper intuition in this matter is the fact that one cannot imagine oneself as ceasing forever to exist — as being totally extinct — even though one may actually think that this is the case. Subconsciously everyone has an awareness of the imperishable element existing at the core of one's being. It is in fact a bonafide spiritual intuition. However it becomes submerged, or is rationalized away, by the materialistic mind.

Going to sleep and dying can be equated in many ways, the real difference being that with final departure, the so-called dead can not return

*World Poll: Int'l Research Associates, as reported in New York Herald Tribune March 23, 1958

to the physical vehicle. The living individual, during sleep, goes into the astral world every night, meeting experiences there which are remembered, if at all, only in the fragmentary and dissatisfying ways of dreams. He returns to the physical body every morning. Therefore he does not go into an unknown realm when his physical body dies. Were this fact more widely recognized, many anxieties would be relieved concerning death as a strange and totally foreign experience, an ultimate fearful fate. If he is possessed of sure intuition, or of direct first-hand knowledge, death at its proper time can be greeted as though it were a blessing serenely arriving, and welcomed joyously.

The second observation to be made concerning death is that the experience itself is not the painful, fearful occurrence that is usually pictured. It is true that the approach to death often is painful, but with its arrival pain ceases. And unless there is some unusual reason for it, fear is not present. Frequently, however, we are subjected to the idea of death as a final agonizing and desperate struggle, the dreaded ending of all. Many have been the fear-producing versions created about this subject by uneasy minds. These envisionments, however, are not what normally happens.

Let us review what usually occurs, as witnessed by investigators who have been able to observe the transition with awakened higher faculties that are latent in everyone.* The individual who is conscious during his dying hours will be aware of the growing coldness and inertness in his extremities, as the vital life forces withdraw toward the heart center and the region of the brain. Normally, during this period there takes place a flash review of all that has been experienced in the life now closed. This swift playback of one's life-track, the micro-filmed history, as it were, of one's entire life, all of its contacts and events, the capacities developed, the powers unfolded and limitations incurred, is the final act of a process that has been operating throughout life — that is, the recording of a person's every experience upon one single physical atom, termed the *permanent atom*. It is so named because this single atom is retained by the Soul throughout the whole series of lives that is necessary for the human stage of evolution. Contained within the permanent atom is the Soul's total vibratory capacity in physical matter. By

The Other Side of Death by C. W. Leadbeater

means of it the Soul returns to the physical plane life after life, each time in a mortal body that is precisely adapted to his requirements. This aspect of the subject embraces one of the great ideas that together assembled, render Theosophy's concept of reincarnation soundly reasonable and logical.

FREEDOM — LIGHTNESS — BUOYANCY

As the dying person proceeds through the withdrawal stage, he is suddenly aware of standing aside from the dense physical body, fully conscious in his vehicle of subtler etheric and atomic matter. However, he has not yet departed from the physical world. His familiar surroundings are visible to him — the pictures on the walls, the furniture in the room, his body lying on the bed. He can see those who may be present at his demise. His first realization is most likely to be that he certainly is not "dead." When one steps out of the physical body at death, the immediate awareness is that of freedom, lightness, buoyancy. There is nothing to fear about departure from the physical body. Pain has been reduced to a minimum by science; and the average experience of transition, more often than not, is a happy one as many indications testify. It should

LET GO---AND WALK INTO THE LIGHT

be revealing that usually the dying person's face relaxes, and frequently lights up with a smile, ofttimes becoming radiant as with some inner glow of vision. If knowledge were more widespread about the mechanics of death and the general course of events, people's anxieties would be greatly relieved; and those who have passed on would understand their situation when they try futilely to communicate with friends on the physical plane only to find that they cannot be heard or seen. With knowledge, the late-departed would realize that they are now embodied in subtler, etheric matter and cannot expect to continue contacts in the usual ways. This experience which might ordinarily be disconcerting is not, because one's attention in that solemn hour is deeply attracted elsewhere. Usually one has relatives and friends who have already passed on to realms beyond the grave. Through ties of love they are present to greet the arrival on the other side. Perhaps one has been a person of deep faith and devotion, and the great Teacher toward whom he has aspired is present in some glorified form to help him upward. The whole experience is that of looking upward, stepping up, moving onward, out of the earth life now ended. If one is scientifically minded and examines his situation, he

might see that the "silver cord" that has linked his
living consciousness to its physical form throughout his life on earth has broken; the flow of prana
through his etheric double to the dense body has
ceased. He may also see that he, himself, now in
a subtler body, is the consciousness that has united
the physical form with its vital life forces — he is
the Immortal who is departing. The corpse that
remains is but a mere collection of independent
cells. The moment the etheric vehicle withdraws,
worth — and prana ceases to circulate, the cells — their
molecules and atoms struggling to separate —
begin to break down the hitherto well organized
physical body.

Normally after death the individual stands
aside from his body, experiencing a brief lucid
period of full awareness and general relief about
the event, before he falls into the peaceful sleep
that intervenes between this stage and his awakening in the astral world. The situation is akin to
imagining yourself as dying upon a bed of pain,
then suddenly becoming aware of being not only
on that bed, but simultaneously elsewhere, moving about light-heartedly across some upland
meadow, in the mountains, let us say, on a sum-
mer's afternoon, with the warm sunshine and
fragrant breezes caressing you, and your whole

being thrilling to a rapture of color and harmony; and by merely imagining it, you are able to supply your every need. Moreover, here you discover old friends who have been gone from physical life for many years; and perhaps, too, yours is the happiness of encountering yet more exalted experiences. Would you want to come back to the painful limitations of the physical world? It would be only natural that your greatest urge would be to make every effort that calls forth from your inmost being the creative powers of Divine Will, and Universal Love, to purify and wash away all that is selfish and cruel, unlovely and ungracious, in order that you may enter more and more the glorious worlds and inner life of the Soul.

THROUGH THE ETHERIC SHEATH

So we depart from the physical world, clothed and conscious in our sheath of etheric matter. The transition into the astral world should be swift, and usually is. This may not be true, however, for the person who tries desperately to cling to the physical world and its desired objects, even though these are fading into a gray insubstantiality. Such individuals find it to be literally true that everything is there, visibly surrounding them, but "you can't take it with you." Those persons who have inordinately enjoyed their possessions in privileged environments, and whose lifelong preoccupation has been to exploit their advantages, are not going to relinquish the position if even a semblance of it can be clung to. Not intending to let go, they clutch at the figment of their earthly condition, being thereby gripped in an unsatisfactory contact with the physical world. The prospect is gray and drab, as can be imagined, if we remember that the etheric is a shadow-world of the physical plane. When you recall that human consciousness in its physical body is vibrant with life in three worlds simultaneously, the mental world with its continuous thought activity, the astral world of feelings and desires, and the physical, with its variety of stimuli, it is but natural that the color and contrasts of consciousness in the physical world seem infinitely more real than in the gray half-world of etheric matter where consciousness is deprived of its faculties of creative thought and physical expression. A clinging person has his total consciousness focused in the etheric sheath that links the physical and astral regions but is not fully in either one of them. Thus he is temporarily *earthbound.* Anyone in this condition will remain so for as long as he is driven to hold on at all costs to what remains of his earthly estate.

As an aside, it might be useful to suggest here that the existence of the etheric sheath of matter, between the physical and astral planes, explains certain puzzling phenomena met by those scientists who are exploring frontier states of human consciousness by physical means. The new techniques of isolating a subject from all sensate stimuli for periods extending over many consecutive hours, or even days, is an attempt to investigate, step by step, under laboratory conditions, the ranges of human consciousness that remain when divorced from all sense impacts. The resulting experiences are being classified as conditions of hallucination and illusion. These experiments, of themselves, will result in further establishment of the materialistic view of life, because logical conclusions are that a continuous stream of impacts upon the senses, together with the responses of the physical body and brain, are necessary for normal, healthy, integrated living. It follows that sensate consciousness structures reality and, conversely, that any departure from it tends to unreality and unbalanced psychic states. A knowledge of the planes of nature suggests that the subjects of these experiments are encountering phenomena connected with the etheric counterpart of the physical brain and with the etheric realm.

Death, however, is complete removal from all sensate impact and consciousness. It is, in other words, a departure into conditions of reality that are experienced through means other than sensate. That such conditions actually exist is evidenced in numberless testaments found everywhere throughout the cultural history of mankind. Theosophical accounts of life after death have described these conditions with confirmations through direct investigation. Such explorations have made it clear that the experiencing of life's Reality in subtler realms far exceeds the limited aspect of it experienced on earth. It is this happy discovery that crowns the great adventure of discarnation, the first steps of which transport us through the etheric veils of matter. The informed person knows, as does the simple man of faith and devotion, that the way to die is confidently to let go of this world, and just as confidently to relinquish the etheric shell that links one with it. This is accomplished simply by not clinging to the world being left behind. Ordinarily there is no awareness at all of the etheric vehicle, because within a few moments or hours after death, deep and peaceful sleep intervenes before entrance into the astral world. The etheric condition would not require attention given it, except for the present-day overriding emphasis upon the material values of life. Dying from this world is made to appear as an event of ultimate misfortune. Consequently there is likelihood of unnecessary suffering due to earthbound bewilderment. Instinctively a knowing person lets go and looks upward with aspiration, toward higher realms, toward the sublime objects of his devotion, and *walks straight into the Light,* leaving this mundane sphere with a fond *au revoir,* and his blessings upon those remaining here. The result of this relaxed condition is the natural falling asleep that has been mentioned as preceding awakening "in his place" in the astral world. His place is where the surroundings and conditions reflect the kind of life he has pursued on earth. The period of sleep may extend but a few moments, or it may be days, or years, and sometimes longer as the case may be, before the etheric matter is disentangled from both the dense physical and astral worlds.

ASTRAL SOJOURN

The after-death life in the astral world has been referred to as the "Summerland" in many Spiritualist communications received from those who have passed on. This is a poetic allusion to the comparatively tranquil atmosphere that pervades this interesting condition and the changes that are taking place in the individual. When the principle of disenthrallment that lies behind the astral sojourn is understood, the conditions to be met with there are readily reconstructed. The total cycle of an incarnation includes not only the Soul's coming forth into new mental, astral and physical bodies, but also the periods of disassociation from them. The disentanglement of the desire nature, the astral energies, from identification with the physical world is the main business of the stopover in the astral region. Obviously the time spent there varies with the intensity of one's recent enthrallment in physical materiality. The conditions, too, vary infinitely in accordance with individual cases. The utterly coarsened creature, befouled and malignant, will find himself after death situated in the lowest and densest regions of the astral world (said to be contiguous with and slightly below the physical plane)* sur-

*See *The Astral Plane* by C. W. Leadbeater

rounded by the creations of his own desires and cravings. He will remain in this region as long as there are energies in his nature having an affinity with it. Boredom with the prospect will bestir the soul in due time even here, to shuffle off the heavier astral coils and progress by major effort into a brighter, happier world. The people who are not involved with the worst elements of life on earth, but who were nevertheless entirely earthy in all that they responded to, after death will awaken in an astral situation that befits their outlook. It will have an earth plane background, because this portion of the astral plane is nearest to duplicating the physical world.

Obviously, a web of sensual and vicious feelings becomes a serious imprisonment in the lower astral worlds. Clairvoyant glimpses of such conditions by mystics and occultists down the ages have given rise to the number of vivid descriptions of hell and its accoutrements that have reached us via various teachings. While it is certainly true that some individuals have managed to inherit an after-death state that is remindful of the most extravagant accounts of damnation, their melancholy situation is not eternally prolonged. Also it must be remembered that in each case the individual soul is immortal; and even though his recent efforts on earth may have turned out badly, and his life has been a dismal failure, he is not thereby doomed to eternal hellfire. More accurately understood, the individual is cleaning away the debris during his astral plane readjustments in preparation for fresh opportunities and renewed efforts when he returns to earth at a later time.

The term "Summerland" seems appropriate as a designation for the average person's astral plane situation. He finds that even though his desire nature while on earth may have generated a certain bondage to physical satisfactions which continue temporarily in a more intensified form during astral life, there is, accompanying all this, a wonderful release of unfulfilled desires of a higher nature. Suppose that a person, while on earth, always wanted to paint or sing or dance — to express joyously and creatively in some way, the beauty and love that he has envisioned and felt, and that he had no opportunity to express — nothing now will prevent him from turning his full attention in such directions. Compared to the physical, the astral world is a place of exhilarated consciousness. One is engaged in a metamorphosis of one's nature from the relatively mediocre condition of the life on earth, into a closer resemblance to the god-like nature of the Inner Self. The process of etherealization educes every possible intensification of the refining impulses and freedom-generating characteristics that have been awakened in the astral nature. There is a stepping up of the emotional life to highest levels. It may be recalled that every facility of the astral world invites creativity. One creates naturally and readily in astral matter, for it is mobile and plastic and responds instantly to feeling, thought and will. Creative people — artists particularly — can anticipate the delights of unhampered inventiveness and expression of beauty through original impulses.

From the limitations that beset us in physical form, there has now come release to relatively limitless, free expression of feeling in astral matter. There is still limitation in the sense that everyone is limited by the desire-habits and emotional patterns that have been his customarily during the lifetime on earth. With these encasements shattered and swept away, the liberations that follow seem miraculous. There are innumerable cases such as that of the individual hobbling about on crutches for many years prior to his death, who continued for a time in his astral body to think of himself as a cripple, and therefore plodded along on astral crutches. He needed to be told: "Friend, you no longer need those crutches— you don't even have to *walk* to get where you are going!"

How do you move about in the astral world? Simply. You visualize clearly where you are going; then you *will-desire* — and you are there!

In the astral world the individual is learning to use his divine powers in a more direct way than was possible in the physical body when on earth. The process of education and growth continues in the astral life at an increased pace. Each person advances through association with one service group and another, through various cultural bodies, and from school to school, learning to release more of what he really is when he is his best self, learning to serve with selfless motivation in this realm of freer expression. All are discovering the great secret of astral life, which is that wealth and richness lie in giving the self in service to the surrounding world, radiating the Inner Light and Life so that they flow *through* oneself. There is no longer need for self-aggrandizement for "getting somewhere in the world." Anxiety and fear regarding the necessities for survival are foreign to this place. With the death of the physical body, food and shelter, fine clothes and a new automobile, cease to be of any concern. The sharpening pressure of the astral life is the preoccupation with being delivered of the coarser elements of the desire nature that inhibit the flow of spiritual vitality. Education of the finer aspects of one's emotional capabilities has the continuous attention of the dweller in astral regions. All of these conditions indicate that variations in time periods are required by different individuals for this experience. Each moves through it according to his capacities; some linger for years, other less evolved and more primitive people remain there for centuries between incarnations.

But as wonderful as the astral life turns out to be for the majority of people, the prospect that lies beyond them is still more splendid. Progress continues into higher astral plane regions until the last earthly ties are dissolved and all links with its pain and sorrow are ended. Then one drops into a serene sleep while final disengagements from astral matter take place. Following this, one "dies," so to speak, from the astral world to be born in heaven, or "Devachan," as it is often referred to in theosophical literature. *Devachan* means literally "the abode of the gods" — that special portion of the mental plane where discarnate humanity enjoys total rest and recuperation between incarnations.* Before proceeding into an examination of the heaven world, let us give consideration to certain abnormal post-mortem situations.

THE EARTHBOUND MATERIALIST

The materialism that prevails in almost every level of life today doubtless is increasing the number of the disembodied who are having to cope with earthbound difficulties. The term earthbound designates the individual whose life and outlook were confined to physical horizons, and who is either unwilling to approach, or is incapable of entertaining, any meaningful ideas of existence divorced from earthly sensate experience. Such a person will have major adjustments to make in departing from earth-life as has already been indicated. Instead of falling into the normal sleep that accompanies death, he finds himself outside the physical body fully conscious of the physical surroundings. He knows he is not "dead" and can only deduce that he is in a body of some kind, apparently a replica of the one there on the bed, but with a difference. In a misty, befogged way, the physical world is about him. For want of

*See *The Devachanic Plane* by C. W. Leadbeater

CLINGS TO DESIRED OBJECTS

something else to do, he will attempt, in all likelihood, to engage in customary activities. Due to
his fixed notion that there is no life after the death
of the physical body, his problem is that his whole
attention is turned earthward. Nothing else is im-
aginable. He cannot let go of what he has known
and wanted, even though it appears now to be
but a desolate shadow of the real. Due to the tran-
sitional function of etheric matter acting as a
bridge between the physical and astral worlds,
two-thirds of his consciousness is inoperative. His
responses are confined to the instinctive, repetitive
reactions of the etheric matter that was connected
with the physical brain during its lifetime. The
brain, of course, is dead. Motivations issue from
automatism. The person is not in pain, but likely
to be miserably unhappy and lonely, and fearful,
too; fearful of leaving the position he finds himself in because he does not believe that there is
anything further on. Although he knows he is not
dead, there seems to be nothing ahead of him but
return to earth. The usual physical objects are
there but they are *different*. He may walk up to a
living person to touch him on the shoulder and his
hand will pass right through the physical form,
or if he speaks to him he will not be heard. He
realizes that he is not visible. Entering the living

room he finds that he cannot move a chair or a table, but he can sit down in his usual comfortable place. Because of his completely fixed idea of this experience, he can readily reproduce it, automatically sitting in a physical chair in his etheric body. A living person may come along, however, and sit right through him in the same chair! To his astonishment both are occupying the same space with no contact whatsoever between them.* This is highly disconcerting to say the least. If he were in command of all of his faculties, he might easily assume that he must be mentally deranged. The earthbound person, in many cases, can be assisted; not always however, because often it is the depraved individual, or one possessed of a savage nature and overpowering sensual drives, who becomes inextricably welded to physical matter. The condition must run its course, wearing out the compulsive force before he will be able to receive assistance.

Those who can be helped need re-direction; need to know where they are, and what is happening; need to know that there are freer realms to look toward. Fortunately even the materialistic-

*Since finer grades of matter permeate denser levels, any number of increasingly subtler planes may occupy a given point in physical space. In order to move from one level to another, consciousness is increased in vibratory velocity rather than transported somewhere else in space.

ally minded person loses interest at last in clinging to the physical world, in trying to contact it. No one living pays any attention to him; so he turns, in due time, away from the attachments that have bound him. Sinking into sleep, he leaves the gray loneliness and awakens in the astral world to a happier condition where new relationships, as well as teachers and helpers, will assist him, and where there is the prospect of endless progress toward spiritual heights beyond.

Unfortunately, much of the testimony about life's continuance beyond the grave that comes to us from invisible realms through channels that contact living entities there, proceeds from those sources nearest the earth plane. Very often the communicants are earthbound souls with less than anything of value and significance to share. Indeed the position is reversed, for they themselves are in need of assistance. Their offerings are not likely to encourage one's enthusiasm for anticipating a similar fate, nor are they helpful in formulating any realistic idea of the state in which consciousness continues after separation from the physical brain and body.

It is a dismaying fact, that whenever wide popular attention is centered on some communication that has apparently been established between physical and super-physical realms, and that seems to confirm the soul's immortality, the conditions that are depicted are anything but desirable. People are introduced to the most sublime concept that is in the possession of man; namely, *evolution toward perfection through the process of reincarnation,* by being presented with an earthbound desiccated version that can only repel intelligent and thoughtful individuals. Visionless and without grandeur, rebirth becomes a return from an aimless wandering in dreary limbo to this physical world of sorrow. Anyone with spiritual sensibilities rejects such testimony knowing intuitively that the inner Reality is ever radiant with beauty and splendor, and with power that unfolds Godward. Death's secrets have hardly begun to be revealed with passage through the first gateway from the physical plane. Only when the enlightenment of all the inspired revelations of the Founders of the world's religions, of the saints and seers and sages of old, has become the integrated Wisdom of mankind, illumining experiences of men everywhere, in this world and hereafter — only then, can there be a steady vision of man's sublime nature, of his future of splendor; only then, may one command a spiritual perspective that stands universally true in every direction.

DEATH THROUGH LEGAL EXECUTION

Among those who are earthbound will be found the criminally-minded and violent-natured victims of capital punishment, as well as those others who may not be criminals, but are among those who nevertheless were condemned to death through some form of legalized execution. These unfortunate persons, at the time of death, are forcibly ejected from the physical world, usually gripped by intense feelings of fear, horror and hatred, and sometimes filled with a violent thirst for revenge. Who dies in this condition, without love, finds himself clothed in his etheric body, amidst ugly and dreary surroundings, confused and bewildered. The best possible thing for him to do at the time of death is to make the greatest effort to keep his thoughts centered upon the highest and noblest aspirations of which he is capable. If there is someone whom he loves, let him feel that love in the greatest, purest possible measure. This effort and feeling will remove him far from the condition into which he is precipitated at death, into a state of peace and the sleep that precedes awakening in the astral world. Those who are unjustly incarcerated and condemned to death through error, or the cruel malice of another, can bear this misfortune patiently in the knowledge that universal law unerringly returns to each soul the fruits of his acts whether they were committed in this or in former lives.* Old accounts become balanced at the appointed hour. Only further unnecessary pain can result from feelings of hatred, intense resentment and a desire for revenge. It is more intelligent to try to understand the episode in some context of gladness that this "debt to the universe" is being paid in full, that what was *taken* from life somewhere in some cycle is now being *given* to life, through the working of the Law.

The violent, passionately natured individual will, of course, be fully intent upon continuing the kind of indulgence he has sunk into. He feels driven to return to his usual haunts and now that he is free to do so, he will try to repeat his customary experiences. If perchance he was slain during a criminal assault of some kind, he is projected in full consciousness into a state where he is free to continue his action, although he is without physical contact. The craving for sentient experience is so intense that he is automatically drawn to attempt it vicariously through the consciousness of a living person with whom he can

*See *Karma,* by Annie Besant

establish some kind of rapport. Inevitably he is drawn toward living persons with inclinations similar to his own, especially to those who are subject to his influences, because they are psychically unstable and emotionally immature. He gravitates naturally to vicious atmospheres, to locales of iniquity, of evil purposes and of excessive indulgence in physical passions. His urges can become monstrously elemental, with no rein upon them, and a hapless individual upon whom he has fastened, and has possessed is rendered capable at such times of any savagery and violence, however brutal. The psychically insecure person, especially if youthful, frequenting places of vice, invites this kind of possession. Psychic possession is also invited by those unstable individuals who indulge abnormally in repeated visualizations of evil atmospheres and actions, as can readily happen in these days of cheap publications and forms of visual presentation that offer an unending array of sensual and violent experience. The elemental and possessive influences that are thus attracted can add the final motivating impulse to crimes of delinquency and violence. Persons with pathological tendencies toward crime need to be recognized as such and institutionalized for treatment. When some act they have committed is a capital offense, the offender should be incarcerated for training, not legally ejected into the etheric world to become another invisible marauder to fasten upon weakened and similarly inclined individuals on earth. Society in its ignorance creates these forces and can only cope with them blindly and ignorantly.

THE SUICIDE

The population of souls that are bound to earth's locale after death is increased by those who commit suicide. Despondence, fear or boredom — whatever the motivation—the suicide has reached an end of his endurance, and despairing of the prospect ahead, has resorted to self-destruction. Unfortunately he lives to regret it. He discovers too late that he is not just a physical body whose consciousness will disappear like a candlelight when the flame is extinguished. Alas, he learns that he *cannot* die! The natural span of an incarnation on earth is apportioned by the Immortal Self, and the contract cannot be suborned by the mortal personality without incurring limitation. The situation would be akin to the hand or the foot deciding for itself that, desiring to live no longer, it would resort to self-amputation. The

THE SUICIDE *fortunately can be helped*

person thus deprived, would live on, of course, minus the deserting member. In the total frame of a human being's life, the lawful ordering of one's members rests with the Great Arbiter, the Immortal Self.

Instead of solving his problem, the suicide only intensifies its worst features; he places himself under disadvantages which he would not deliberately choose were he in possession of Soul-knowledge. Not adequately realized is the service rendered in times of emotional and mental stress, by the relative inertia of the physical body. Its heavy responses slow down the astral storms of passion and desire; its routine demands and rhythms break through the patterns of psychic compulsions. Very often physical necessities and their preoccupations bring surcease to mounting tides of feeling. Lunch-time and a chat with a friend often serve as a brake-pedal for some thrashing psychic compulsion. Deprived of the assistance rendered by the physical body in resolving a situation of stress, the individual who commits suicide simply hurls himself into an astral vortex which is an enormous intensification of every psychic torment and fury that drove him to self-destruction. His is no enviable position. It would have been better to "sleep on it;" to have had another look at the situation in the morning; to have talked to someone about it; or to have prayed for guidance. The escapee who has chosen to interrupt his natural span of life will now spend the remainder of it in the gray etheric corridor between the astral and physical worlds. Relief for him lies in surcease from the cycling, repetitive storms and pressures of feeling. These will wear away in time, but they are somewhat like the movements of a body in frictionless space; they require time, or counter impulses to change their course.

Fortunately, the suicide can be given assistance from the physical world as well as from the other side of death. Influences are needed that will alleviate the tensions, permitting natural forces to relax the condition of turmoil. Love is the great creative power at every level of life, and if the suicide has been well known and loved by someone, that person is in the best position to render assistance, surrounding the unfortunate one with healing thoughts of sympathy and well-being. Through compassion and with knowledge, the aid of healing angels can be invoked. The person trained in meditation can do even more: he can invoke the inner Divine Light to irradiate the victim's atmosphere with forces of love and peace that tend to still the tumult or depression and aid him in awakening his own inner spiritual powers and sense of direction toward his place in the astral world.

SUDDEN ACCIDENTAL DEATH

Finally, among the specialized cases where post-humous conditions are not normal, is that of the victim of sudden accidental death. A person ejected from his body while fully conscious and engaged in some kind of action at the moment of death is likely to continue his activity temporarily, not realizing he has been killed. This is true because his astral body has become disengaged from the physical body, with the entire etheric sheath intact, which means that all the astral and etheric matter contiguous with the physical plane still surrounds him; consequently, he is fully aware of the physical world though it is beginning to assume queer aspects. Fortunately the unpleasant situation is not prolonged and is soon transformed into a condition that is consonant with the character and nature of the person, as well as that of the experience through which he is passing. Those whose earth lives have been kindly, dutiful and peaceable, naturally have no affinity for coarser, violent or more gruesome atmospheres, and from such their consciousness simply fades away. The selfless, noble-minded individual, becomes immediately oblivious to all that is transpiring around him in the disaster in which he has met death. He goes at once into a state of quiet, harmonious sleep that lasts until he awakens naturally in the higher astral or heaven world to which he is drawn. Between the two after-death extremes, that of the fully earthbound person, and that of the advanced individual detached from worldly attractions who goes at once to higher realms, there are as many types of post-mortem adjustments as there are individuals and situations.

A principle that is active in all cases is that, as man lives within himself, so does he die; he carries through the gateway of death the full inner content of his life — its most potent element, that of his motivating aspirations. Another point to be cognizant of in all deaths, and especially the shockingly violent cases, is that physical pain is impossible from the instant the *silver cord* is broken. This is the thread of specialized life-matter that links higher consciousness with the physical body throughout an incarnation. From the moment this link is snapped, the individual is "dead" to the physical world. As long as the cord remains intact, it is possible for one to return to the physical body, becoming conscious in it again.

Any one of us may encounter sudden death in a wreck or a calamity or when merely walking along the street. This latter kind of experience befell the author in a manner so violent as to involve all the factors of sudden death at a moment when consciousness, by contrast, was fully engaged with preoccupations at the opposite extreme of violence. Because this occurrence has documentary value with reference to the subject under consideration, perhaps the following personal account of its significant features may be usefully introduced at this point.

The accident took place on a paved highway upon a cold, sunny afternoon. The wind was blowing so that my coat collar was turned up causing all sounds to blend with the rush of wind in my ears. I was walking along the shoulder of the road facing traffic, if there had been any. No car was in sight when, crossing the road, I began my return journey. In a quiet, happy state of mind, deeply engaged with perceptions of beauty in the surroundings, I was completely unaware of a car that was now swiftly approaching from the rear. Its driver was asleep at the wheel, and the

.....WHERE DEATH IS NOT

automobile was edging over to the wrong side of the road and onto the shoulder where I strode along with no slightest premonition of impending disaster. Suddenly, with unabated speed, the car struck my body, smashing my legs with its bumper, head and shoulders with its radiator and hood, then flinging the body some fifteen feet along the road to land head first on the pavement where it slid to a rest. As far as I was concerned, the body had been violently killed while in full and free action, and while I was mentally focused in regions of abstract awareness. Unconsciousness continued for several days, with life in doubt, while the body was in the hospital.

This detailed description enables me to give full weight to the categorical statement that there was no experience whatever of pain, no slightest ripple of fear or horror, no agonized feeling of any kind. I had been intently preoccupied with perceptions of beauty and the deep sense of joyousness that usually accompanies such contemplation, when suddenly personal consciousness disappeared into boundless universality. The merging was instantaneous, with no awareness of blankness or blackout, only of transition into a shoreless ocean of Life and Light, an unobstructed Wholeness, radiant with love and power unending. The arresting factor was the unbroken sense of self-identity. Without bewilderment or anxiety, with only the clearest assurance that *death was not,* I was alive in a universe of Light. There, streams of Divine Force are seen raying downward into the worlds below, and at the physical level every living thing is seen channeling these radiations of Light. Apparently every flower, tree, animal and man has evolved its physical body as a perfect anchorage in physical matter for radiating these forces that are constantly influencing and changing the world about us. Although my consciousness during the period of coma was located in the higher realms indicated, I found that I could descend at times into the physical brain to deliver some communication. But in each instance, consciousness returned at once to the formless world where it was centered. The center was there, not here in the brain and body. Even though the *silver cord* was not broken, consciousness was performing as though it had been reoriented as a result of death.

The sojourn which I am describing lasted for several days, during which it became clear that man cannot live fully and continuously in that awesome region until he has awakened and unfolded his consciousness to cosmic proportions.

The growth to godhood is a gradual process, requiring ages of evolutionary effort, of innumerable relationships that call into expression every potential of love and lawful being. How precious, then, becomes each relationship with family and kin, with companions and associates, and with all whom we actively contact, friends and enemies alike. Each one challenges some additional aspect of our nature, evokes some new facet of our capacity to love and to understand. No less important in this unfoldment of the inner Divine Self, are the relationships we have with Nature, with all living creatures, each radiating some measure of the totality of forces which compose the ocean of Being in which we exist and share in the One Life of God. All relationships throughout time are assisting in the awakening and unfolding of each individual's latent powers, his capacity to dwell forever in Omniscient, Omnipresent Consciousness. Reasonably disposed, therefore, is this school of life in which we reincarnate in changing patterns of relationship, sometimes as husband and wife, again as child and parent, or brother and sister, pupil and teacher, disciple and Master — and in all these many wonderful ways discovering together the higher dimensions of Divine Love and Cosmic Consciousness.

During the several days that were spent in this profound retreat, a change took place in the mysterious depths of my consciousness. Movement earthward seemed to begin with an urge toward further sentient experience. The center of consciousness moved "downward" level by level as in the process of reincarnation, reaching at length, and becoming established again in the heavy brain and body. I found, then, that it was possible to journey in thought and being to where I had been, but the center of consciousness was now changed, anchored in the physical form, returning to it from whatever excursions were attempted. Having "reincarnated" so to speak, there followed a curious period of reluctance to resume interest in the illusionary pageant of earth life. (The most insistent impression brought back from "outside" physical existence is that of perceiving the completeness of our state of illusion while blanketed in the physical body.) The perspectives that give meaning to every detail of life had been opened, however, and these provided fresh motivation for effort.

The personal experience just recited seems to confirm several important points that have been noted previously as we have reviewed the subject of death and the conditions immediately following. For one thing, the whole cycle of the human situation was clearly etched: the reincarnating Self was known in his own realm by the instantaneous leap of consciousness to its highest abode at the moment of its release; then in due course was experienced the "thirst," or need for sentient existence that institutes the process of reincarnation; following this, there was a conscious return into the limited personal outlook, sheltered in its carapace of flesh, submerged in the ocean of material illusion.

The illusion is complete mainly as a result of our instinctive identification of consciousness with the physical body and material world. How natural it is for us to be certain that we see with our eyes and hear with our ears — together with the brain centers with which these organs are connected, physiologists will add. There is no questioning the fact that anyone deprived of eyes and ears can no longer see and hear. If there is report of a blind man who can "see" in another way, or of a deaf person who "hears" in some extraordinary manner, this is interpreted as some form of sublimation of physical reality, if not of imagining, or hallucination. At all events, it cannot be normal sight and hearing, therefore cannot be equated with reality as physically sensed.

It is here that the illusion of matter takes hold, for we mistakenly identify all of reality with sensate experience. Throughout time man has commonly measured real existence in physical terms. But human consciousness, in the course of evolution, is evolving subtler awareness of reality and contact with it in greater and lesser measures. Even now it is understandable that the senses of sight, hearing and touch are merged in a *super-sense* of "magnetics," of identification through vibratory rapport, or resonances. We employ a number of terms to report such consciousness. The words harmony, empathy, unity, and the inclusive term *love,* used in its universal, unobstructed meaning, all indicate a super-sensing of Reality (here denoting Universal Being and Becoming, the manifestation of Absolute Truth.)

With the death of the physical body, consciousness, released from identification with sense-reality, does not simply disappear into nothingness, or into some condition associated with flimsy imagining. Consciousness "goes" magnetically to the level of reality in which it is already centered, The magnetics are fixed at all times whether we are "living" or "dead" — fixed by the sum total of consciousness of the Self in its mundane and universal regions of being. These realms of the

Self are most reasonably set forth in the comprehensive theosophical conception of the seven principles of man.

What has been said here appears to have validity in view of the experiences accompanying the accident described above. For example, there is the strangely significant fact that my consciousness was never anywhere near the scene of the accident, not even momentarily. It continued to be where it was oriented at the moment of the accident: namely, in an abstract formless region of the inner worlds where joyous unity prevails. From this, it follows as an inevitable implication, that we go, after death, where we already are in our inner life. Heaven and hell are states of consciousness that we create, and have the power to recreate. Many thinkers have said as much.

Another point inviting attention is that my state of consciousness not only had no traffic with the physical scene, but by-passed similarly, both the etheric and astral conditions — in fact, every level of form. Here illustrated, it seems, is the importance of one's outlook at the moment of death. Death approaches each one, offering the greatest opportunity of the whole incarnation for one to rise into, and sustain, a high peak of realization, the effect of which will surely benefit subsequent conditions. This observation gives significance to Tibetan ideas concerning the opportunity that is available to everyone at the time of death. Their ideas will be found especially interesting to the reader who is giving careful attention to the subject.* According to Tibetan custom the administering priest seeks to enjoin in the dying person an achievement of the highest possible level of consciousness in meditation, and the sustaining of it just prior to the moment of death. The effect of this willed effort is to project the person at once, after death, into the sublime life of the Immortal Self.

A final point to be mentioned because of its theosophical connotations, is the lasting result, of the experience related above. This can be described as a state of "high-tension relief," that is to say, of relief as to the wondrous life surrounding us and stretching limitlessly ahead of us, to be realized in ever deepening measure; therefore, the total needlessness of the anxieties and fears that beset us as to our ultimate fate. The term "high-tension relief" is meant to indicate a condition of keyed-up awareness, of energized volition, that slides back the imprisoning canopy of physical limitation, and breathes the air of

*Tibetan Book of The Dead: translated by W. Y. Evans-Wentz

conscious immortality. The effects permeate all levels of the lower self with a spreading sense of *relief* and of reattunement with that enduring quality which in nature is recognized as timeless patience.

Let us turn now from considering abnormal after-death situations and renew our main theme of tracing man's path through death and after. We had reached the condition of departure from the astral world, and the soul's advent into heaven. This "second death" involves separating the last of the astral matter that was entangled with mental matter during the incarnation. Throughout a lifetime of habits and practices, certain mental matter in a person becomes completely identified with lower astral feelings and desires. Strong, passionate personalities, with self-centered drives, render a large part of their mental energies subservient to their astral natures, thus creating a vigorous *desire-mind* complex that governs their lives. This desire unit is so involved in an individual's life problems that it has been classified in theosophical literature as one of the vital principles of man: the *kama-manas,* from *kama,* a sanskrit word meaning "desire" and *manas,* "mind," "the mind of desire."* It is the energetic element

*See *Seven Principles* by Annie Besant

that expresses "I want," "I must have," etc. The desire-mind factor is indeed the transient personality that gradually dissolves and disappears during the after-death stages. It has no permanency as an entity, but the good and evil acts wrought through it during physical incarnation do persist as causes that will have future effects and will be inherited by the soul in a subsequent time.

During the interval of falling asleep at the close of the astral period and prior to the awakening in the mental or heaven world, the last of the separation of matter of the two planes takes place. The astral *permanent atom* alone is retained from the now abandoned astral corpse, which is in a state of slow disintegration. As in the case of the physical permanent atom, the astral permanent atom will remain attached to the Immortal Self to be used in the future when a new astral body will be constructed with exactly the same potentialities and capacities that the last one had. In each of the three worlds, physical, astral and mental, the permanent atoms store the total vibratory capacity that has been developed by the soul throughout the ages of his evolution in those levels of matter. Once more we can note the provision of machinery for developing human nature steadily towards perfection.

HEAVEN IS INEVITABLE

We arrive now at the closing and longest chapter of the cycle of incarnation, the return home to heaven. This is the most beautiful and inspiring part of the Soul's heroic pilgrimage through birth and death. And it can be stated as a matter of fact that *heaven is inevitable*.* Everyone goes to heaven, but of course not all portions of his nature can reach there. Astral desires that were identified completely with satisfactions in physical matter have been left behind. They are "dead," and will not enter heaven. But a person's

The heaven periods between incarnations are not to be confused with the eternal state of bliss and omniscience entered by one who has become liberated through achieving union with Divine Spirit and passes beyond the human stage forever.

101

astral desires that expressed unselfish love and other elements of his higher nature will be very much a part of the heaven life. Heaven is inevitable, because the Immortal Soul, dwelling in his center in the highest division of the mental plane, radiated his energies into lower worlds, building three bodies, the mental, astral and physical, and now, following the incarnation, proceeds to disassociate himself from them. His longer repose in heaven is necessary for mental disengagement from the past incarnation. The length of time he spends there, and the measure of his experience, will depend upon the richness or poverty, as the case may be, of his mental and higher emotional life on earth. The heaven life seems to be mainly a condition of effects, the causes of which were set in motion in physical incarnation. The content of the experience is unique to each individual. But in every case it is a blissful period of rest and refreshment, of review and renewal, the full working out of all the highest aspirations he had on earth. While one is in heaven, no link remains with the physical plane across which pain, sorrow or evil of any kind can reach one. Yet friends and those whom one loves, as well as all of the beauty and glory of nature, are present in their cherished aspects in this place of peace where no want or affliction of any kind exists.

One awakens in heaven, his whole being suffused with glorious light and happiness. Transcending all imagery is the continuous delight in mere existence in a region where understanding is gathered through love, where knowledge is ever deepening into wisdom. The Soul's evolutionary function while there is to transmute past experience into faculty, and achieved skills into innate talent. Again as in the physical and astral worlds, all of the experience during the recent lifetime, together with the results of the review in heaven, are recorded upon the *mental permanent atom*. Thus the harvests of one lifetime are carried over as seeds into the next incarnation. In heaven the Soul is actively engaged in elaborating in mental matter great plans and visions to be developed on earth. Many are the forms of transcendent beauty and power, or enterprises of brave proportion successfully achieved on earth, that have been worked out in the preceding heaven-lives of the geniuses responsible for them.

Each individual takes into heaven that which is native there; all of the unselfish thinking that he has initiated, all that he has expressed on earth of the good, the true and the beautiful goes with him. These are the thoughts and deeds that are as heavenly wealth, to be explored in every avenue of meaning, their essences extracted and processed into mental character during the profound contemplation that takes place.

Students sometimes make the mistake of viewing the heaven-life as altogether illusionary, a period of unwanted withdrawal from the scene of action, the physical world, where evolution is proceeding at white-hot intensity. They compare the driving necessity for action on earth with the reported tranquillity of heaven-world existence and perceive only the kind of inactivity that is associated with boredom here. The anticipated "stillness" repels rather than attracts many spirited, vital people. Everyone knows, however, that the most sublime achievements of man, as well as the greater joys that any of us have while on earth, come through concentrated mental or other inner effort that requires comparative stillness of the physical body.

Let there be no misunderstanding about the mental plane as a scene of action! It should be realized that the Soul is relatively more active there than when physically encased in a body. Action is far freer in mental matter. There is continual change of occupation in the heaven-world, just as much and more than on earth. The difference is that the heaven world occupations are always pleasant, filling the hours with rapture. The frustrated aspirations during earth-life are fully attained in heaven, not simply prolonged but completed in all their infinite developments that flow out of each incident and aspect.* Life on earth yields the rough ore which the Soul smelts, forges and tempers into tools and instruments that will be put to use in the next earth life.

We lay up treasures in heaven by our many and varied contacts, by the breadth and depth of our interests on earth, by what we revere and support here with willing hearts, striving to serve the wise and not the foolish pursuits of life. It is understandable that the more evolved individual will make better use of the heaven life, for he is more fully the immortal Architect, envisioning in the deep silence of the mental world his plans for future creations.

In due season, even the heaven period draws to its close. Since the time spent there is measured by the spiritual content of an individual's earth-life, there is a closing phase, and definite termination to the heaven periods between incarna-

*See *Death – and After?* by Annie Besant

tions. When finally the last impulse from the past incarnation has run its course, the transient personality has completely disappeared. Perhaps a thousand years have elapsed since the person died. Nothing now remains of the lower vehicles; the physical body and its etheric sheath disintegrated centuries ago, along with the abandoned astral shell; and now the mental assemblage has been used and harvested. The Soul no longer identified with the limited edition of itself, either as man or woman, withdraws into the eternal aspects of the Self centered imperishably in regions beyond the heaven world — the true paradise of the spirit — where he knows himself as the God he is. From this sublime height he can look backward and forward outside of time, glimpsing the Great Plan and the part he is playing, and is destined to play, in its gradual unfoldment. The vision unveiled in him contains within it the goals and objectives of his next life on earth. As some guiding star it will shine in the inmost, silent sanctuary of the Soul throughout the incarnation. Hence the intuitive person, "true to himself," is enabled to make right choices throughout a lifetime toward the fulfillment of soul purpose.

VISION OF THE IMMORTAL TASK

From the inmost region of the Soul, motivation toward rebirth commences; the intent arises for further sentient existence, and the forces are gathered to be tried in the fires below.

The Soul, refreshed and strengthened in ability and purpose, is fully prepared to come forth again into physical life. At the appointed hour the descent begins. First to be accomplished is the creation of a new mental body. This begins with activation of the mental permanent atom, charging a force field in mental matter, into which are attracted by magnetic affinity mental atoms that respond exactly to the vibratory rates that have been evolved and recorded upon the permanent atom. The new mental body is an exact replica of the last one regarding its potentialities and capacities.

On the next level below, and in a similar manner, the new astral body is created. Meanwhile activities have commenced on the physical plane. In order for one to grasp more clearly what takes place in the creation of a new physical body, two major factors must be considered. A knowledge of them provides at once a clarifying frame of perspective in which to view such questions as:

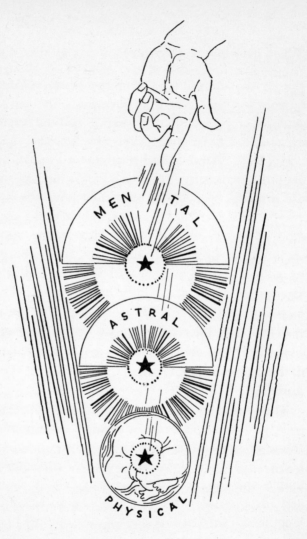

PERMANENT ATOMS ACTIVATED – *Reincarnation Begins*

What determines parentage, race and sex? Circumstances of birth? When does physical birth begin? When does the soul enter the baby body and take possession of it? If there is a *plan* for the incarnation, why the sorrowful accidents of birth, the crippled, distorted and sometimes monstrous shapes that occur? These and many other questions are presented to the reasoning, orderly mind by the concept of reincarnation.

The two governing factors mentioned above are first, the *life plan* of the Immortal Self — the objectives to be sought, the great goals and purposes that are now possible in the forthcoming life. This pattern of forces accompanies the Soul and will act as a pull of the future throughout the lifetime. This life-plan is innate with the shape of things to come. An instance is the sense of destiny that has marked certain outstanding individuals.

The second of the two factors is the *inheritance from past lives.* This will act as a conditioning frame of limitations built into the new physical body. The inherited characteristics are transmitted under operation of the universal law of cause and effect known widely as the "Law of Karma." Here it will be useful to shed a theosophical light upon this ancient but misunderstood term.

THE LAW OF CAUSE AND EFFECT

Karma is a Sanskrit word meaning "action." In a metaphysical context it links action with reaction as a natural cycle of cause and effect. The law that it designates is often referred to as the Law of Readjustment, or Law of Equilibrium, that is ever restoring balance in the physical world and broken harmony in the moral world. H. P. Blavatsky considers it to be the *"Ultimate Law* of the universe, the source, origin and fount of all other laws which exist throughout Nature.*"* She explains that "Karma is the unerring law which adjusts effect to cause, on the physical, mental and spiritual planes of being . . . intelligently and equitably each effect to its cause."

When we consider that effects linked to their causes are instituted in cycles that extend through time, and that many of them reach beyond the demarcations of birth and death into other lifetimes, the light of reason penetrates otherwise inexplicable situations that man encounters on earth. All that has ever been initiated or enacted by him in the worlds of form, that has resulted in good or ill, remains linked to the Soul and destined for readjustment. In the course of time

The Key to Theosophy by H. P. Blavatsky: Section XI "What is Karma?"

112

all forces are brought to equilibrium by the operation of universal law. Right action is equilibrated by happy conditions; evil, by evil inheritances.

The Soul returns to earth amidst the woven pattern of karmic forces that he has himself generated. He is engaged upon an immortal task to which he is awakening amidst the fires of matter. Out of the heritage of causes he has set into motion in former lifetimes on earth, appropriate segments are apportioned by laws operating through higher spiritual agencies, and precipitated to be dealt with during the Soul's lifetime. This is the inheritance that is referred to as "one's karma." Karma is not understood in its positive meaning when it merely designates an overshadowing inexorable fate, a predestination about which the individual can do nothing. Such notions overlook the law's creative beneficence as an educating, liberating provision of life. Within the framework of karmic law, a man creates his own destiny, works out in time his own salvation, and wins his way to the freedoms of immortality.

KARMA AND CREATION

The creative aspect of the Law of Karma is simply visualized in the illustration on the opposite page. As conceived here, the upper figure represents the real situation of every human being as standing in the hand of his Divine Creator who envisions and wills the perfect universe to be achieved. The Great Plan of life is unfolding by means of the universal adjustment of causes and effects. The cyclic law through which all things are created is represented as the rainbow of forces arising behind the upper figure who is sowing seeds of good works, feelings and thoughts with one hand, while with the other he is scattering pebbles and stones of discord and disharmony, of cruelty and violence. As he does so, he creates the rainbow of forces that sweep outward in a lawful spiral of attraction-repulsion, a tide of forces that meet the figure below, who is the same soul in a later time encountering the effects of his own earlier action. His path has been roughened by the barriers of limitation he has created, and it also has aspects that have been made lovely and gracious by the good and beautiful acts performed and service to Truth rendered. A general recognition of this law would restore to humanity its lost sense of spiritual self-reliance.

The karmic pattern that is inherited by each individual, therefore, is a governing factor in the process of reincarnation. It determines when he

Destiny tomorrow will rule; Man's will is today's tool.

will be born, in what kind of a body, and under what circumstances, who the parents will be, with whom there will be close relationships, what greater persons, teachers, friends there will be a possibility of meeting. The law does not withhold, rather it supplies the conditions by means of which the Immortal Soul can create, by remote control, the "divinity that shapes our ends." Knowledge of the working of this law in its positive aspect affords one of the freedoms of conscious immortality. For with a growing awareness of self-identity extending through time and into the Eternal, an individual meets gladly, either the limitations or liberations that are precipitated by the karmic law. Each condition brings further self-knowledge, releasing some fragment of the divine potential within. There is both alertness of mind and tranquility of heart in knowing that

"Destiny today is master;
Man was master yesterday.
Destiny tomorrow will rule;
Man's will is today's tool."

No single lifetime of an individual is isolated from his other lives. Each life is the child of all the preceding lives on earth and the parent of those that follow it, all of them together the continuing existence of the individual.

All forces deriving from the two factors, the Soul's life-plan and the inheritance of karma, merge in the creating of the physical body, its appointments of parentage, race, place and hour of birth, together with the pattern of limitations and assets that will unfold in the individual's life.

The machinery by which these conditioning forces are translated into physical form is focused in the physical permanent atom. When it is activated, the force field, generated in the etheric levels of the physical plane, attracts streams of subtlest matter into an etheric vehicle that begins to form. This has been referred to previously as the etheric double, because it is in fact a model of the physical body that is to be built, a living blueprint. Within this mould the baby body is constructed cell by cell, as it gestates in the mother's womb. The physical permanent atom has reached the womb through either the father or the mother, depending upon which one has the strongest link with the soul that is coming back into birth.

Clairvoyant observations of the period of pregnancy reveal that from the moment of conception, birth begins; the zygote and permanent atom emit together the "sound," or vibration that commences to produce the mould in etheric matter.

To understand more fully the exquisite care and skill which Nature exerts in every lawful way to protect and facilitate the building of its forms, one must enquire of the available records of clairvoyant research into the angelic and elemental kingdoms of life. Certain entities from these kingdoms are vitally active in the creation of any living form.* Along with these invisible intelligences at work during the gestating period of the human baby, the reincarnating Soul actively affects the streams of matter drawn into the mental, astral and physical forms and implants his own vibrations upon the particles through a shaft of white light that plays between his center and the permanent atom centers of his new mental and astral bodies and into the heart of the fetus. At the moment of fertilization, this shaft of light de-descends from the soul heights into the spermatozoon, irradiating it with energies that will set in motion the processes mentioned above. These energies are released and procedures are begun the moment that an entity is formed by the combination of the positive and negative forces of the spermatozoon and ovum.**

*The Kingdom of The Gods by Geoffrey Hodson.

**The Miracle of Birth by Geoffrey Hodson.

RETURN TO EARTH

At length the baby body is ready for birth and is borne into the world. The Soul arrives on earth, encased in its new vehicles, "trailing clouds of glory" but heavily immersed in matter, with memories of heaven and his true estate fast fading. His full attention now is drawn to the incessant stream of sensate impacts within and upon the physical body. His response capacity is assisted by the body's animal instincts, as well as by faint stirrings of latent potentials in the new astral and mental bodies. All of these will be slowly awakening as educational effort and training proceeds. Very much depends upon the order in which these built-in capabilities are brought forth. The surrounding cultural norms will play a decisive part in educing latent faculties and fixing their patterns as governing forces in the individual's life. A wider knowledge of the true nature of man could provide more certain guidance, a surer sense of direction in developing methods of preparing the child for more skillful living in the modern world.

Rejection of the idea of reincarnation on the grounds that "no one remembers his past lives" cannot be sustained in the light of the knowledge of the laws of its operation. The simple truth is that we do not remember in usual ways because we inherit with each lifetime new astral, mental and physical bodies, and there are no patterned grooves of cells and atoms, no machinery of recollection in the new personality directly linked with former incarnations. If by chance, or by some obscure resonance, such a groove does happen to occur, consciousness flashes with a hazy memory of having "done this before" or having known "this place" or that "circumstance" previously. But memory is prevalent in many so-called instinctive responses experienced by everyone. If one wants to remember fully, effort must be undertaken that is aimed at a break-through into Soulknowledge. This treasure of immortal knowledge becomes increasingly available as one awakens *conscious immortality*. Twentieth century beliefs in general are contrary to such an outlook. Anyone who would approach direct knowledge of the Immortal Self, must stem the usual currents of thought, the bright lights of popular notions, setting out courageously to follow the dim star of spiritual intuition. Often it is during investigation of the fields of metaphysical ideas that the first experiences of true Soul-memory occur. A sustained effort to project thought into these realms results in a growing awareness of the Self extended in time — an extension that reaches beyond the walls of birth and death that confine us in a single incarnation. Flashes of intuition from the deeper levels of consciousness reveal ranges of hidden splendor of Inner Being, more glorious than have yet been described or expounded in the systems of philosophy and religious faith. To open the individual path inward is the most exalted of human endeavors, one that crowns every age of mental freedom and enterprise.

THROUGH IMMORTAL CONSCIOUSNESS TO SPIRITUAL KINGSHIP

With the birth of the baby, the Soul, now reincarnated, treads again the age-old path of joy and sorrow that stretches to the far heights of human perfection. The winding road presents a changing panorama of illusions that test and try the Soul. How otherwise than by the beneficent blackout of reincarnation might the Immortal Self gain complete mastery of his vehicles of force and form? With repeated plunges into the abyss of matter, he learns amidst darkness to see the Light; in the midst of despair to move with indomitable courage; in times of fear and indecision to be steadfast in purpose, clear as to the direction of Reality; and where all is change and death, to know himself as changeless, imperishable Being.

The ancient and noble concept of reincarnation, of the spiraling growth of the Soul, level by radiant level, toward some far-off, perfect Day-that-is-to-be, has a beauty of design, a grandeur of proportion, that appeals to the highest intuition and reason of man. Who embraces its philosophy is thereby freed from the burden of unknowing that blinds mankind to greater service. His heart at peace, he is able to awaken perception that sets him upon the path to liberation. With dauntless patience and undisturbed conviction, he can begin to evoke even now atmospheres of harmony, by absorbing within himself the conflicts and dissensions of daily life, the embattled elements that surround everyone, recreating these with his vision of the Truth and Beauty that dwell at the heart of all things. Joyously, then, as an Immortal

He unites himself with Those who labor to lift life